SHIRE NATURAL HISTORY

LIZAR
of the Briti

CW00958250

PETER STAFFORD

CONTENTS

Cover: *Male Sand Lizard from Dorset.*

Series editor: Jim Flegg.

Copyright © 1989 by Peter Stafford. First published 1989.
Number 46 in the Shire Natural History series. ISBN 0 7478 0028 6.

Printed in Great Britain by C. I. Thomas & Sons (Haverfordwest) Ltd, Press Buildings, Merlins Bridge, Haverfordwest, Dyfed.

Introduction

Wherever the climate is warm and sunny there are sure to be lizards of one sort or another. Basking on a wall or scurrying across a footpath, they are a familiar sight abroad, even in towns and around houses as many a visitor to the Mediterranean will have noticed. The small, quick-moving and often brightly coloured creatures we may see on holiday are fairly typical of lizards in general, but the family as a whole embraces species of many sizes and forms, ranging from small, elongated legless types which burrow into the earth to the huge dragon-like monitor lizards. Also included within the group are such bizarre and unusual kinds as the tree-dwelling chameleons, with their extraordinary powers to change colour, the geckos, which can hang upside down from the ceiling, the flying lizards, which have expansions of skin between the limbs for gliding, the poisonous Gila Monster and the seaweed-eating marine iguanas.

There are altogether twenty or so families and approximately three thousand different kinds of lizards, the greatest majority of which occur in the tropics, decreasing in numbers with distance from the equator. They are all classified as a suborder (the Squamata) of the order Sauria, which also includes the snakes, and like snakes the bodies of lizards are covered with scales. Unlike snakes however, all lizards possess movable eyelids and external ear openings, by which even the most snake-like legless species can normally be identified. Also, the two halves of the lower jaw are not loosely attached at the chin as in snakes but firmly united. Many lizards also show differences in sexual colouration, and their tongues vary greatly in shape and character.

Lizards are typical ectotherms. They are unable to generate their own body heat voluntarily and instead maintain their temperature through behavioural means, basking in the sun and absorbing heat from their surroundings, their skin being a good thermal conductor. Of their different senses, probably the most essen-

tial is that of sight. The majority of lizards are chiefly insectivorous and need keen eyesight to be able to chase and catch their prey, often at speed. Some lizards have a pineal or 'third' eye situated beneath a transparent scale on the top of the head, the primary function of which is thought to be as a photoreceptor. The lizard's sense of hearing is also quite sharp and, with a middle ear, is better developed than in most other reptiles. The ears, however, are sensitive only to a rather narrow range of frequencies, with low-range sounds being most easily detected. Also important to lizards is a keen sense of smell, for which, in addition to the olfactory membranes of the nose, they have a specially modified structure in the roof of the mouth known as Jacobson's organ. As with snakes, in which the structure is best developed and most sensitive, particles of scent are picked up from the surroundings and conveyed by the tongue to the palate, where they then pass through a duct to Jacobson's organ for 'tasting'.

The lizard has a typical reptile skin covered with scales, and within the different groups there is considerable variation of scale types. The topmost epidermal layer of the skin needs to be shed every so often to allow for growth, and the frequency with which this occurs depends on a range of factors including age and intake of food. In most cases the skin is shed in fragments, being rubbed off amongst vegetation, against a stone or other abrasive surface; it may sometimes be eaten by the lizard. In the Slow-worm (*Anguis fragilis*), however, it is often discarded in one piece, much like snakes, peeling over the back from the snout and turning itself inside out.

In their skeletal anatomy the lizards differ somewhat from each other according to their particular way of life. Burrowing forms often have a more heavily ossified skull for pushing through the soil, while in terrestrial or tree-dwelling species much of the cranial structure is cartilaginous and relatively light, giving greater flexibility for feeding on larger items of live prey. The rest of the lizard skeleton generally takes the form of a typical four-limbed vertebrate, comprising a backbone, framework of ribs and

2

four limbs with five toes, the fourth of which is usually the longest. In burrowing and semi-burrowing species the limbs may be greatly reduced or, as in the case of the Slow-worm, even vestigial, but however rudimentary they may be there is always some internal evidence of a pelvic girdle. The vertebral column in lizards is very flexible and may consist of several hundred individual vertebrae.

Several families of lizards, including the two in Britain (Anguidae and Lacertidae), have the ability of voluntarily discarding the tail when seized by a predator. This evolved as a protective mechanism, enabling the lizard to break free if it is caught by the tail and leave it behind to distract an enemy while it makes its escape. To facilitate autotomy, as this process is called, the bones of the vertebral column at the base of the tail and their associated muscles have become specially modified. In most cases the fracture occurs through a vertebral segment and not between the vertebrae, and is brought about by contraction of the muscles, which the lizard itself is able to control. After fracture a new tail grows back, although it is never quite so long or well formed as the original. In regenerated tails the vertebral column is replaced by a cartilaginous rod and the scales are darker in colour. Extraordinarily, two or even three new tails may sometimes develop from the point of fracture when a tail has been broken. A regenerated tail can still break again, the fracture occurring across the next vertebra up.

Like the snakes, male lizards possess a paired reproductive organ, each part of which can be used independently of the other. It lies in the base of the tail, where it can be seen as a distinct swelling. During copulation the part of the organ in use is turned inside out like the finger of a glove. Fertilisation is internal. Most lizards are oviparous, producing eggs with a tough parchment-like shell, although there are a few, including the Common Lizard (*Lacerta vivipara*) in Britain, where development of the embryo is completed in the oviduct and the young are born alive. The number of eggs or young varies according to species and age of the female.

In terms of communication and social behaviour, lizards are the most advanced of all the reptiles. The way in which they respond to different circumstances and the methods of communication they adopt vary considerably between species and the sexes. The behaviour of males towards other males in defence of territory, for example, especially in the breed-

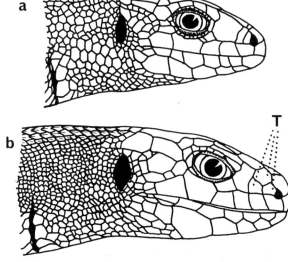

1. *Pattern of head scales in (a) Common Lizard (Lacerta vivipara) and (b) Sand Lizard (Lacerta agilis). Confusion may sometimes arise in distinguishing between these two species in the field, especially juveniles, but where there is doubt the Sand Lizard differs in always having a 'triangle' (T) of three scales behind the nostril.*

3

ing season, is frequently violent and may include bobbing movements of the head, dramatic changes of colour, open-mouth displays and direct physical contact. Some species are also able to communicate by sound. Geckos in particular are well known for the noises they can make and many other lizards, including a British species, the Sand Lizard (*Lacerta agilis*), have been heard to utter high-pitched vocalisations. In response to an enemy lizards may inflate their bodies, thrash their tails and make various other threat displays. One group of species, the horned lizards (genus *Phrynosoma*), have developed the unusual ability to squirt blood from their eyelids as a defence strategy.

Although many kinds of lizard are brightly coloured or have the ability to change their colouration, most species are patterned in a way that makes them extremely difficult to see in their natural habitat. Some kinds, such as the slow-moving chameleons from Africa and Madagascar, have come to rely entirely on their ability to change colour and disguise themselves amongst the leaves and branches, although even those which also depend on speed to escape from predators or catch their prey are often extremely well camouflaged.

Native lizards

There are only three kinds of lizard that can be considered native to mainland Britain, the Slow-worm (*Anguis fragilis*), the Common Lizard (*Lacerta vivipara*) and the Sand Lizard (*Lacerta agilis*). After the glaciation of the last ice age, these were the only three to advance north from the warmer parts of Europe across the English Channel, which at the time was an area of dry land, and establish themselves before being separated by the invasion of the sea. All three species are found over much of Europe as well as in the British Isles, and the Common Lizard in particular is one of the most widely distributed of all reptiles, ranging eastwards over large areas of central Asia to northern Mongolia and the Pacific coast. A fourth species, the Green Lizard (*Lacerta viridis*), has

flourished on the Channel Island of Jersey since it broke away from continental Europe. It also occurs on Guernsey but seems unable to survive and breed on the British mainland despite attempts to introduce it. This species and the Wall Lizard (*Podarcis muralis*), another native of Jersey as well as a successfully naturalised immigrant in southern parts of Britain, are dealt with separately in the next chapter.

THE SLOW-WORM

The Slow-worm, or Blind-worm as it is sometimes called (both rather inappropriate names for a creature that is neither a worm, nor blind nor particularly slow), is the most easily recognised lizard in Britain. With its long cylindrical body and lack of obvious limbs it differs significantly from other native species and can even be mistaken for a snake, although it is identifiable as a lizard by its closable eyelids and easily broken tail. Its body is less supple than that of a snake and also rather hard to the touch due to a layer of protective bony plates under the scales. The scales themselves are larger on the upper surface than on the animal's sides and are perfectly smooth, giving it a highly polished appearance. The Slow-worm has no discernible neck; its head is small and rounded and the top of it is covered with rather large symmetrical plates. In adults the tail is longer than the head and body combined and ends in a short spine. One of the longest Slow-worms found in Britain, a male from the London area, measured just over 460 mm, but most average between 300 and 380 mm in length.

In their skeletal anatomy Slow-worms differ from virtually all other lizards in possessing only vestigial remnants of the pelvic girdle and hind limbs. Their internal organs are also elongated and arranged in a somewhat displaced manner to suit the narrow shape of the body.

Like many other lizards, the sexes differ somewhat in colouration. Adult female Slow-worms are essentially brown, reddish-brown or copper-coloured, with blue-black sides and a dark vertebral stripe which is in most cases retained from infancy. Males, on

4

2. *Male (below), female (above) and baby Slow-worms (Anguis fragilis).*

3. *A male 'blue-spotted' Slow-worm.*

the other hand, tend to be greyish and more uniformly coloured, usually without but occasionally with a greatly reduced vertebral stripe. Males also have slightly larger heads. There is not a great deal of variation in colour and pattern within the British Isles, but occasionally adult males may be found with blue spots on the upper surface. This, however, is more a character of the species in the eastern part of its European range. The blue spots do not begin to develop until about the third year of life and may vary greatly in number and size. They may also disappear at any time, leaving brown spots in their place. Newborn Slow-worms are exceptionally attractive, being golden-yellow, greenish or silverish above with dark sides and a bold dark vertebral stripe. With increasing age this bright colouration is gradually lost, although in females the contrasting vertebral stripe and dark sides never seem to disappear completely. Some females may also have two rows of small dark spots arranged longitudinally on each side of the vertebral stripe, which sometimes fuse into continuous lines, and irregular flecking on the sides. The ventral surface is dark grey or blue-black in both sexes.

The Slow-worm leads a different and more secretive life than other British lizards. It is fond of basking and in the early morning will lie out in the sun for long periods, especially in spring, when mating is under way, or in late summer, but it seldom exposes itself completely, concealing itself amongst leaves or matted grass. For the greater part of the day, however, it remains hidden under rocks, fallen logs, in holes in the ground, buried beneath leaf litter or even in ants' nests. Slow-worms are excellent burrowers and appear to be just as much at home underground as they are above. Between late afternoon and dusk they emerge from their hiding places in search of food, which mainly consists of soft-bodied invertebrates such as slugs, worms, spiders and various insects and their larvae. They may also eat snails, teasing them out of their shells before swallowing them, but are perhaps most partial to the small white slug *Agrolimax agrestis*, which will often be taken in preference to other types. In searching for food the Slow-

worm moves slowly and purposefully amongst the ground vegetation, pausing every now and then to 'taste' the air with its tongue. When a meal is located, the head is raised and pointed directly down at the victim, which is then seized suddenly and either held for a short while or chewed from end to end before being swallowed. Slow-worms are often more active after rain, when the slugs and worms on which they mostly feed are easier to find.

Slow-worms do not take to water as a matter of habit but can swim well if they have to. On land they move in a graceful snake-like fashion, sometimes with surprising agility. If the ground over which they are moving is particularly smooth they will often push the tail spine downwards into the earth for extra leverage and then 'hitch' themselves along with the chin. When first caught they may struggle for a short while and discharge the contents of the cloaca but very rarely attempt to bite and usually settle down quickly when handled. If a Slow-worm is seized by the tail, however, at least part of the appendage is almost certain to break off. After a while the fractured stump heals over and may show some degree of regeneration, although the tail never seems to grow back as well as it does in the other British lizards.

The Slow-worm is one of the most widely distributed of all reptiles. It ranges over most of Europe eastwards to the Ural Mountains, the Caucasus and parts of south-west Asia and also occurs in north-west Africa. In the British Isles it occurs almost everywhere except in Ireland and the Orkney and Shetland Islands and is the only reptile known on the Outer Hebrides. It is essentially terrestrial in habits and generally favours well vegetated dryish country with extensive ground cover, such as open heaths and commons, although it can also be found abundantly in rather damp areas. In the south and west of Britain it is often to be found on steep cliffs by the coast and may also be encountered in woodland clearings, on old ivy-covered walls, hedgebanks, railway embankments and even in gardens. One of the best places for finding Slow-worms during the day, sometimes in considerable numbers, is

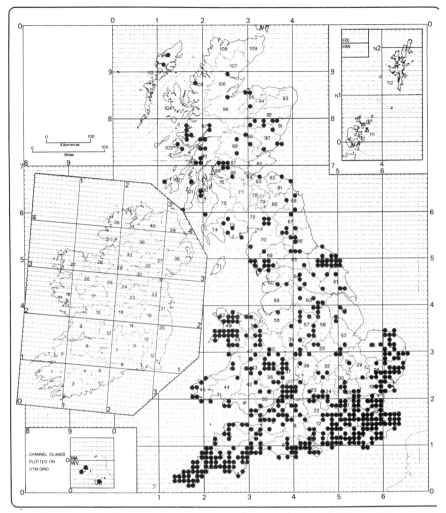

4. *Distribution of the Slow-worm in Britain (records cover the period 1960 to 1985).*

under sheets of old corrugated iron left lying on the ground, where the temperature usually remains higher even when there is little or no sun.

The Slow-worm can live for a remarkably long time, its length of life exceeding that of all other lizards. There are many instances of Slow-worms living for up to thirty years, but the record is held by one in the Zoological Museum, Copenhagen,

Denmark, that lived to be 54 years old.

THE COMMON LIZARD

Lizards of the family Lacertidae, to which all of the remaining species in Britain belong, are highly developed and, in evolutionary terms, the most advanced of their kind. In Europe, especially around the Mediterranean region, lacertids, or 'true lizards', as they are fre-

7

quently known, are by far the predominant species of lizard and occur almost everywhere in a profusion of different forms. Some species are so alike they can only be identified by their scalation. With the exception of a few large species, most are rather small, measuring less than 8 cm from snout to vent. They are by nature a group of alert, opportunistic and quick-moving lizards, active by day and very fond of basking, even when the temperatures are quite high. All have a typical lizard shape with a long tail and well developed limbs, and many species are brilliantly coloured. Some species show a high degree of sexual dimorphism, males usually being more colourful, especially in the breeding season, and sometimes also larger. In the character of their scalation lacertid lizards are all quite similar; the shields on the top of the head are enlarged and are symmetrically arranged, and the body scales on the back are small and keeled, while those on the sides are smooth or only slightly keeled. On the belly they are significantly larger and arranged in a regular series of longitudinal rows, and on the tail they are strongly keeled and set in transverse whorls.

In common with many other families of lizards, lacertid species of both sexes possess femoral pores or glands, set in a single row on the underside of the thigh. These secrete a waxy substance consisting mostly of cellular debris, the biological purpose of which is not absolutely clear, but it is thought it may provide a means by which males, which produce more of the secretion in the reproductive season, can mark their individual territories with scent. In adult males the pores themselves are also much larger and, by their roughness, may play some part in helping them to remain coupled with the female during copulation.

Quite the most familiar native species, commonly seen all over the British Isles, is the Common or Viviparous Lizard, a rather drably coloured species but exceptional in that, unlike other lacertids, it bears living young. Adults grow to about 6.5 cm in length from snout to vent with a thickish tail up to twice as long, rather short legs and a smallish, rounded head. In colouration the Common Lizard is essentially brown, reddish-brown, olive or greyish, but the pattern may vary considerably. The male is usually darker on the back with scattered but distinct pale-centred spots, or *ocelli*, while the female is paler, usually with a broken vertebral stripe, a few scattered *ocelli* and a number of light streaks on the sides. Specimens may occasionally occur which are quite green in colour and may be mistaken for Sand Lizards. The throat is whitish or bluish. In males the underside is yellow, orange or reddish, peppered with fine black spots; females may also have a few black spots but more often the underside is plain yellowish-white or bluish-grey. In this and other species of

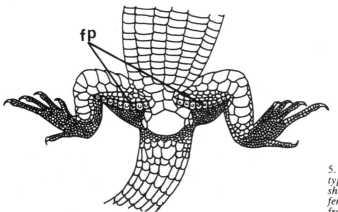

5. *The underside of a typical lacertid lizard showing the position of femoral pores (redrawn from Smith, 1954).*

8

6. *Male Common Lizard.*
7. *Female Common Lizard.*

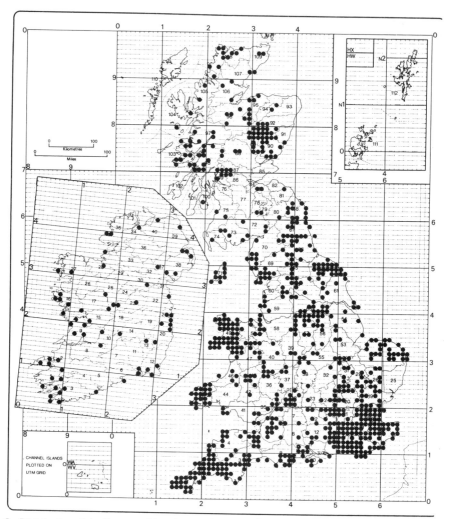

8. *Distribution of the Common Lizard in Britain (records cover the period 1960 to 1985, except for Ireland).*

Lacerta all-black or melanistic individuals may sometimes occur. The young are very dark, almost blackish-bronze, usually with two rows of paler spots down the back.

The Common Lizard is found in a wide range of habitats but on the whole favours slightly damper places than other lacertid species. Most typically it occurs on open, marshy heathland, south-facing banks with a covering of dense vegetation, wasteland, the edges of woodland and in damp meadows, but it can also be found on railway embankments, sand dunes and in gardens. It may also occur on precarious sea-cliffs and even venture on to rocky shores within the spray zone of breaking waves. In common with other lacertids it is fond of basking but dislikes great heat and in southern Europe, where

10

the temperatures are appreciably higher, it is usually restricted to mountainous regions (up to 10,000 feet, 3000 metres, in the Alps). Some individuals have favourite basking spots to which they return every day. In particularly suitable basking areas they may congregate together in large numbers; in his book *The British Amphibians and Reptiles,* Malcolm Smith records seeing more than fifty on about 2 square metres of ground. When basking the body is flattened and tilted towards the sun to absorb as much heat as possible, and they may also lie on their bellies with their legs sprawled out backwards and the soles of their feet turned upwards. The Common Lizard is essentially a ground-dwelling species but is also an agile climber and will scramble up walls, into gorse bushes or even ascend wooden fence posts to bask in the sun. It is not in the least averse to swimming and if necessary will take to water with little hesitation, folding the legs back against the flanks and wriggling the body and tail from side to side in an undulating motion. Moving on land it proceeds in a series of short dashes. Compared to many other lacertids it is not particularly swift but it is always alert and quick to react if danger threatens.

Common Lizards feed mainly on small insects, earthworms and insect larvae, but larger prey may occasionally be taken, sometimes even young of their own species. Large prey is first shaken and battered against the ground and then crushed in the jaws before being swallowed whole. Their sense of hearing is good, and while hunting for food they will often pause to listen for the rustling movements of insects, tilting the head to one side. The Common Lizard and all other lacertid species usually drink by taking in droplets of dew or rainwater from leaves or blades of grass.

The Common Lizard is the most widely distributed of all lacertids and also ranges further north than any other species, up to latitude 70 degrees in Arctic Scandinavia. It occurs over practically the whole of northern and central Europe, extending south to northern Spain, Italy and southern Yugoslavia, and also through much of Asia to northern Mongolia. It is the only lizard in Ireland and occurs virtually everywhere in Britain with the exception of the Outer Hebrides and some of the Western Isles of Scotland.

THE SAND LIZARD

Rarest and most beautiful of the lizards in Britain is the Sand Lizard, a robust, stout-bodied and rather short-legged species measuring up to about 9 cm from snout to vent when full grown, with a tail some one and a half times as long. The head is short and deep, especially in males, and the snout is rather blunt. It also has more dorsal scales across the middle of the body (34 to 42 compared to 25 to 37 in the Common Lizard), and a distinct band of narrowed scales down the middle of the back. In colouring the Sand Lizard is exceptionally handsome and also perhaps more variable than the Common Lizard. Males are typically green or a yellowish-green colour on the sides, which is most vivid in the breeding season, finely mottled or with a varying number of larger dark spots and *ocelli.* On the back there is usually a central dark stripe or a series of dark blotches bordered on each side by a lighter band and another narrower, often broken or incomplete dark stripe. The female is also attractively marked but not as colourful as the male, tending to be greyish or brownish and only in exceptional cases green on the sides. Occasional specimens may sometimes occur which are almost entirely straw-yellow in colour, heavily blotched with black. On the continent of Europe the Sand Lizard shows even greater variation in colour and pattern; specimens of both sexes occur which may be almost entirely green, black, uniformly dark brown or brick-red on the back, with a few darker markings on the sides. In males the underside is yellowish-green or pale blue with fine black spots while that of females is whitish or pale yellow without spots. Newly hatched and juvenile Sand Lizards resemble adults but are somewhat paler in colour with less clearly defined markings and a pale grey underside.

Unlike the Slow-worm and Common Lizard, which seem to thrive equally well in a variety of habitats, the Sand Lizard in Britain occurs only in lowland sandy country and is now restricted to two main

9. *Male Sand Lizard from Dorset. In the breeding season the green colouration on the sides would be very much more vivid than in the specimen shown here (photographed in August).*

10. *Female Sand Lizard from Dorset.*

11. *Female Sand Lizard from Dorset. Note the variation in markings and colouration between this lizard and the one in figure 10.*

12. *Male Sand Lizard from the Southport area of Merseyside.*

13. *Male Sand Lizard from the Southport area, showing a variation in colour from the lizard in figure 12.*

14. *Female Sand Lizard from the Southport area. Both the male and female have slightly different markings and are paler than the Sand Lizards in southern Britain.*

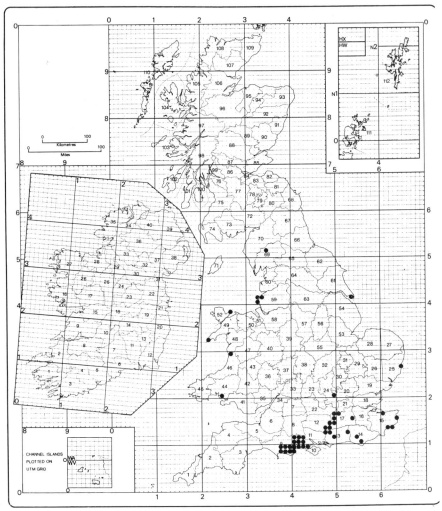

15. *Distribution of the Sand Lizard in Britain (records cover the period 1960 to 1985).*

areas. It is most common on the open sandy heaths of Dorset and Hampshire and the western borders of Surrey and Berkshire. At one time Sand Lizards occurred in considerable numbers on the coast of Kent and East Sussex, but the present status of the species in this area, if it survives at all, is unknown. The only other part of Britain where Sand Lizards still occur is on the coastal sand dunes of the Liverpool and Southport area, although there are now far fewer than at any time in the past. The Sand Lizard is also reported to have been seen in the North-east and other parts of Britain, principally the coastal regions of Northumberland and Yorkshire, although the species does not occur naturally in these areas and confirmed sightings are believed to have been of introduced speci-

14

mens. The Sand Lizards of southern Britain are generally somewhat darker than those from the North-west and have slightly different markings. This may be a result of the different types of habitat they each occupy.

The Sand Lizard is more of a communal species than the Common Lizard and often occurs in colonies. In Britain it may inhabit areas where the vegetation is dominated by large, sparse clumps of marram grass (*Ammophila arenaria*) and other tuft-forming grasses, such as on sand dunes, or alternatively by dense stands of mature ling (*Calluna*) and heather (*Erica*). As a rule the animal is almost always found where there are well drained banks of loose sand in which it can excavate holes for itself. Sand Lizards are habitual diggers and may also make use of abandoned rodent tunnels in which to live, sometimes blocking the entrances with grass, moss, leaves or earth for protection against the cold. Any number of individuals may reside in the same tunnel, using it as a means of escaping danger and as a shelter for the night. On the continent of Europe the Sand Lizard is less restricted in its habitats and may be found in woodland clearings, in hedgerows and even on the edge of cultivated land.

Like the Common Lizard, the Sand Lizard spends a great deal of time basking in the sun, although it too dislikes intense heat and in very hot weather will retreat underground or into shade. In spite of its name '*agilis*', it is a poor climber and quite unable to scramble up vertical rock faces with the same agility as the Common Lizard or Wall Lizard. It is perhaps more timid than the Common Lizard and generally not so easily approached, often diving for cover if so much as a shadow passes over it.

The diet of the Sand Lizard appears to be more varied than that of the Common Lizard and may include fruit and the occasional flower as well as insects of various kinds and spiders. In captivity it has been fed chopped meat and worms, dead bees and their larvae, and even honey. Living prey is usually battered against the ground or a stone and stunned before being devoured. Beetles, grasshoppers and similar prey may first have their hard wing-cases removed to make them easier to swallow.

The Wall Lizard and other immigrants

Since the early twentieth century a variety of exotic lizards have on occasion found their way into Britain, usually accidentally, by escaping from captive collections, but a few species have been introduced deliberately and in such numbers as to form breeding populations. Most of these 'immigrants' have been unable to survive and reproduce under British weather conditions and have usually perished within a very short space of time. Others have managed to establish themselves and survive longer, even for several years, only to be killed off by an exceptionally severe winter. One or two, however, seem to have adapted quite well to the British climate and even flourish.

Of the surviving immigrant species in mainland Britain, two also occur as extralimital natives on the Channel Islands. Quite the most successful of these has been the common form of a group collectively known as Wall Lizards, which occur in a bewildering array of colours and patterns all over central and southern Europe. In its colouration and appearance, the Wall Lizard (*Podarcis muralis*) is superficially similar to the Common Lizard but is slightly larger (up to approximately 7.5 cm from snout to vent) and has a rather more flattened body with a longer tail (up to 2¼ times as long as its body), longer legs and a larger head. There are usually more scales on the upper surface across mid body (42 to 75), a greater number of femoral pores (13 to 27), and the neck collar is also not so distinctly serrated. Ordinarily it is brown or greyish above but may sometimes be olive-green or

15

16. *In heathland areas Sand Lizards frequently climb into the tops of ling and heather to bask, where they are extremely well camouflaged.*

17. *Baby Common Lizard. The young lizards may stay with the female for a short while after being born, although they soon begin to disperse and hunt for small insects.*

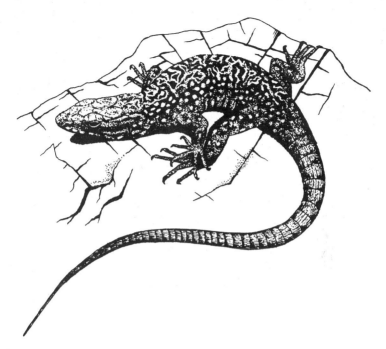

18. Wall Lizard (Podarcis muralis). The male, pictured here, is quite different from the other lacertid species in Britain. Females, however, may look very much like the female of the Common Lizard and sometimes can be distinguished only by the larger numbers of scales (often more than forty across mid body) and less serrated collar. Wall Lizards also tend to have a somewhat 'flatter' appearance than the Common Lizard.

almost completely black, often with conspicuous white bars on the sides of the tail. Adult males may be spotted or have an intricate reticulate pattern on the back, while females usually have a central dark stripe or longitudinal series of spots. The underside in both sexes is normally of a creamish colour relieved by darker spots of red, pink or orange, or black under the throat. Juveniles are rather similar to females in colouration but have a lighter tail.

The Wall Lizard is primarily a species of rather dry, rocky areas and, as its name suggests, is frequently found in the vicinity of old walls and ruins; one of its favourite haunts on the continent of Europe is the old dry stone walls enclosing olive groves and vineyards, which provide ideal shelter and basking opportunities. It is an excellent climber and can

often be seen basking on tree trunks in open woodland, large boulders and precarious rock faces some distance from the ground. Perhaps more than any other species in Europe, it also occurs frequently in and around houses and other buildings, and sometimes even quite abundantly in small towns.

In southern Europe this species is very common, extending from southern Spain, Italy and the Balkans northwards to the Channel Islands, the Netherlands, West Germany and north-west Asia. On the Channel Islands it is found only along the north-east coast of Jersey.

As an immigrant species in Britain, the Wall Lizard appears to be fairly hardy and better able to survive the colder climatic conditions than the various other foreign types that have been introduced. In 1932 a dozen specimens of the nomin-

19. *Male (top) and female Green Lizards (Lacerta viridis).*

ate subspecies *muralis*, the common form in western Europe, were released into a garden in Surrey and took up residence on some old stone walls within the confines of a nearby private estate, where they have remained undisturbed as a thriving breeding colony ever since. In 1954 fifteen specimens of the subspecies *nigriventris* were introduced into south Devon, where they continue to flourish, but a previous introduction in 1937 of some two hundred (subspecies unknown) failed to establish themselves and by 1963 had dwindled to just a few. Two more thriving populations of unknown origin also occur on the Isle of Wight, and another small colony is said to be established in Surrey (Fitter, 1959).

A second species which occurs naturally on Jersey but which has not fared so well in mainland Britain despite several attempts to introduce it is the spectacular Green Lizard (*Lacerta viridis*). Adult

Green Lizards are large, robust creatures, measuring up to about 13 cm from snout to vent with a tail of often more than twice as long. Males usually have a larger head and are bright green in colour, with fine black spots on the upper surface and a blue throat, while females are either brownish or a less brilliant shade of green with irregular blotches or two or four black-edged longitudinal stripes. The underside is usually plain yellow in both sexes. Young Green Lizards are olive or pale brown in colour, lightly spotted or with two or four narrow light lines on the back.

In continental Europe the Green Lizard is to be found in almost any form of habitat well exposed to the sun and with some ground covering of rocks, shrubs and bushes. It is extremely alert and very fleet in movement. In addition to the more usual lizard diet of insects, the Green Lizard will also eat other small lizards, fledgling birds, birds' eggs, and sometimes even fruit.

The Green Lizard ranges over much of western and southern Europe, from the Channel Islands and French coast to northern Germany, south-west Russia and the Balkans. On the Channel Island of Jersey it is said to be widespread and more brightly coloured than in Europe and also tends not to be found in the same areas as the Wall Lizard. A small population also exists on Guernsey at Vallette Cliffs and in the area around Fermain Bay, having been originally introduced from Jersey.

The first attempt to introduce this species into Britain was in 1899, into the Isle of Wight, where it established itself quite successfully and could still be found as late as 1934. Twenty specimens were liberated in North Wales in 1931, to be recorded last in 1935, and a hundred were introduced into south Devon in 1937, surviving as a colony for about nine years. The Green Lizard has more recently been introduced into Surrey, where in 1959 it was said still to survive but not to reproduce (Fitter, 1959).

Over the last forty years or so a number of other exotic species have been introduced into Britain, although with limited success. On two occasions between 1950 and 1960 several specimens of the Italian Wall Lizard or Ruin Lizard (*Podarcis sicula*) and Madeiran Wall Lizard (*Lacerta dugesi*) were liberated in south Devon but soon disappeared and it would seem did not survive. Similarly, a small number of Eyed Lizards (*Lacerta lepida*), released as an experiment into Surrey in 1932, lived only for a short time, although a pair of Moorish Geckos (*Tarentola mauritanica*) set free in a Devon locality managed to survive for three or four years.

Occasional specimens of other species sometimes find their way into Britain, usually arriving from abroad in crates of fruit. Tropical species in particular quite often turn up in shipments of bananas, particularly Anoline Lizards (*Anolis*) from the Americas and geckos of one sort or another. Two species found in a railway goods yard in Cardiff, an Ocellated Skink (*Chalcides ocellatus*) from the Mediterranean and a West African

Gecko (*Tarentola delalandii*) are also thought to have arrived in this way, and it is quite possible that other species may at times escape into the British countryside, although it is doubtful if they are able to survive for very long.

The yearly life-cycle

As 'cold-blooded' animals unable to regulate their own body temperature and dependent largely on the sun for warmth, the British lizards, in common with other reptiles of temperate regions, hibernate during the winter months to avoid the freezing weather. They emerge again in the spring, enticed out by the warm sunshine, although the Common Lizard sometimes appears even earlier and has been seen out basking in February with patches of snow still on the ground. In Britain lizards hibernate from late September or the beginning of October to about the beginning of March, depending on the prevailing weather conditions. Earliest to retire is the Sand Lizard, which in the spring is also the latest to emerge, and it is usually the males and juveniles which appear first. Lizards most commonly hibernate in the ground, burrowing deep into loose earth or disused rodent tunnels, into natural crevices or beneath tree-stumps where the frost cannot penetrate and they can remain safe and dry. Although some may overwinter in solitude, lizards have been known to assemble in considerable numbers and hibernate communally, even in the presence of snakes, one of their main enemies. Slow-worms, in particular, frequently hibernate together and may occasionally be found knotted together in a 'ball' consisting of many individuals.

When they first emerge from hibernation lizards spend much of their time basking in the sun, awakening from their long winter sleep and readjusting themselves once again for active life. During this period they do not normally feed. Towards the middle to end of April the

20. *A Sand Lizard hatching from the egg. The snout of the lizard can just be seen protruding through a slit in the shell. It may take up to several hours for the baby to emerge fully and leave the protection of the egg.*

21. *A day-old baby Sand Lizard.*

males then become interested in mating.

Male Common and Sand Lizards disperse and stake out individual territories, the most aggressive and dominant individuals occupying areas closest to the original place of hibernation. Within these territories a series of routes is established, often through dense cover, which they routinely follow when hunting for food, moving between basking places and their dens, and escaping from danger. Fighting is common at this time and any male trespassing on another's territory is not tolerated, especially in the presence of a female. Of the two lacertids in mainland Britain, the Sand Lizard, being a more socially inclined species, appears to be the most aggressively territorial. When two males of similar size meet they puff out their necks, raise their bodies off the ground on all fours and arch their backs intimidatingly. The green colouration on the sides may visibly intensify and the tail twitches from side to side. If this fails to bring about the retreat of one or other aggressor, one of the males will begin to hiss with its mouth wide open and then make butting lunges at the other, attempting to seize and shake his opponent by the neck. The battle finally ends when one of the males begins to tire and, as it loosens its hold, is quickly chased away by the victor. Serious conflicts are rare, although both fighters may be injured and carry scars about the neck and shoulders for some time.

It is usually the female of the species which locates and greets the male, after which she may be pursued through his territory for up to several hours until at a basking point or other favoured spot the male takes on a more dominant role. The male of the Common Lizard usually mates straight away, seizing the female in his jaws by the head or flank and twisting the lower part of his body beneath hers so that the two cloacas are brought together, but older and more mature Sand Lizard males perform a simple courtship ritual before attempting to mate. This usually takes the form of a short chase, the male eventually seizing hold of the female's tail and working his grasp upwards to her neck, at which point he is able to encircle his body beneath hers to complete the act. Both partners may first raise all four of their legs off the ground as well, shaking the feet rapidly and twitching their tails, oddly enough a form of behaviour sometimes observed when they are alone. As with all species, mating may last for several hours.

Male Slow-worms are rather solitary by nature and do not seem to establish territories or go through a preliminary courtship ritual. They will, however, fight violently with other males for the possession of females, seizing one another by the head or forepart of the body and in their struggles sometimes inflicting severe wounds. The act of mating usually takes place in seclusion, often underground, the male grasping the female by the head or neck and manoeuvring the lower half of his body underneath to bring the cloacas together.

After a few weeks the male lizards begin to lose their enthusiasm to mate and become less inclined to chase and fight with each other, resuming their normal basking and feeding behaviour with the females. The Slow-worm and Common Lizard are ovo-viviparous and produce living young encased in a transparent membranous sack at birth, although at high altitudes in the Pyrenees the Common Lizard has uncharacteristically retained the less protective primitive habit of laying eggs. Young Common Lizards, of which there are usually between five and eight in a litter, each measuring some 37 to 47 mm in length, are born in the months of July and August after a gestation period of about three months. During the later stages of pregnancy the female tends to lead a more solitary life and may become irritable with other lizards, chasing them away if they approach too closely. Prior to giving birth she seeks a damp secluded hollow beneath dense cover, and after the first has been born there may be an interval of several days before all of the remaining offspring appear. As soon as it has been born the young lizard sweeps its head from side to side and pushes forward, rupturing the membrane with the help of its egg-tooth, a small projection on the snout specially provided for the purpose and which is cast off when the first skin is shed. By the summer of the

following year the males become disting-
uishable by their more colourful under-
sides and they may reach sexual maturity
at an age of just 22 months. The birth of
young Slow-worms, which average between six and twelve in a litter, begins in
the middle of August and extends into
early September, although it may be
delayed until October if the weather is
cold. When first born they measure from
65 to 90 mm, growing to about 220 mm by
their second year. Males are said to
become sexually mature in their third
year, females in their fourth or fifth.

The Sand Lizard, in common with all
other lacertids, is oviparous. In June or
July the female lays from six to thirteen
small white eggs in the sand or under a
stone, each measuring about 14mm long
by about 8 or 9 mm in diameter. As
development proceeds they increase
slightly in size and at the time of hatching
may be several millimetres larger than
when first laid. When born the young
measure from about 55 to 63 mm and
may double in size within a year. Within a
short time of birth the young lizards
become fully active and indepdent, hunting and capturing prey with the agility of
their parents.

It is not uncommon to find some lizards
with small, black warts on the softer parts
of their bodies, usually behind the front
or hind limbs. The exact reason why
these appear or what they are caused by
is not fully understood, but it is thought
they may perhaps develop as a reaction to
the activity of skin parasites.

The enemies of lizards, and especially
of their young, are numerous. They are
chiefly preyed upon by hawks, shrikes,
owls and similar birds of prey, as well as
by snakes, rats, hedgehogs and small
predatory mammals, such as the weasel
and stoat, but foxes and badgers will also
feed on them. Domestic fowl have been
known to catch and eat them readily, as
have dogs and cats. Young lizards may
also be taken by shrews, toads, adult
lizards, mistle thrushes, blackbirds and
even robins.

During particularly hot spells in high
summer, lizards may hide away and even
aestivate (go into a state of torpor) for a
short while to escape the heat, burrowing
into loose soil at the entrance of their

dens. The adults will shed their skins
several times, on average every other
month, and in the later weeks of summer
and early autumn preoccupy themselves
largely with basking and feeding in
preparation for winter hibernation. As
the days shorten and the weather grows
colder they seek out a suitable hibernation place, usually underground, and stay
in its general vicinity until it becomes too
cold to remain above ground except when
the sun is shining. Shortly afterwards they
retire for good, remaining dormant in a
state of torpor until the following spring.

Lizards and conservation

With the widespread and increasing loss
of open sandy heathland in Britain, the
numbers of all three native lizards have to
some extent been affected, although
none quite as much as the Sand Lizard,
which is almost totally restricted to these
kinds of heathland areas. The loss of
these habitats can be attributed to a
number of causes, including the rede-
velopment of land for forestry, agricul-
ture, urbanisation and mining, and much
of what remains has also been changed
for the worse by the spread of pine trees
(*Pinus*) and the invasion of other vegetation types such as bracken (*Pteridium*),
birch (*Betula*) and gorse (*Ulex*). The
lizard populations have also needed to
withstand other and more direct press-
ures such as the seasonal burning of their
habitat, predation by domestic cats, the
gassing of rabbit burrows, which are
often used by lizards as places of hibernation in winter, and being collected for
pets. Because of its resemblance to a
snake the Slow-worm is also killed indis-
criminately in large numbers.

It has been shown that the Sand
Lizard, in particular, is rather sensitive to
changes in its habitat and, after a fire or
other major disturbance, is unable to
adapt and recolonise areas as easily as
many other species. As a measure of how
quickly numbers of this species have
declined in Surrey, where in the early
twentieth century they were abundant, it

has been estimated that over 95 per cent of one particular colony has disappeared in a period of only twenty years, primarily as a result of loss of habitat. In recent years, however, considerable efforts have been made to preserve the remaining areas where Sand Lizards occur and to restore the habitat by clearing scrub and exposing patches of sand for the females to lay their eggs. Certain sites have also been repopulated or the numbers increased with captive-bred stock. By managing the species and its habitat in this way, the Sand Lizard has in many areas slowly begun to recover, although as a threatened animal its survival in Britain is still uncertain.

For further protection the Nature Conservancy Council (the statutory government body) has established an advisory group on herpetofauna to prepare and draft national policy on conserving endangered reptiles and amphibians and their habitat. Under the Wildlife and Countryside Act 1981, the Sand Lizard and all other British reptiles are also now protected by law. In an effort to conserve this species and its habitat in particular, it has been necessary to introduce stringent regulations making it illegal to collect or disturb them without proper authority. It is also forbidden to kill or injure either of the two other British lizards.

Useful information

SOCIETIES

The British Herpetological Society, c/o The Zoological Society of London, Regent's Park, London NW1 4RY, produces an interesting bulletin and scientific journal which frequently include articles on British lizards. The BHS Committee for Conservation is the body responsible for much of the work undertaken to ensure the survival of Sand Lizards in Britain.

The Fauna and Flora Preservation Society, c/o The Zoological Society of London, Regent's Park, London NW1 4RY, is actively engaged in conservation issues worldwide. Publications include *Oryx*, a journal of reports on current conservation projects, and *Herpetofauna News*, a specialist newsletter which often has articles relating to British reptiles and amphibians.

FURTHER READING

Arnold, E. N., and Burton, J. A. *A Field Guide to the Reptiles and Amphibians of Europe*. Collins, 1978.

Arnold, H. R. (editor). *Provisional Atlas of the Amphibians and Reptiles of the British Isles*. Biological Records Centre, Monks Wood, Natural Environment Research Council, 1973.

British Herpetological Society. 'The Conservation of British Amphibians and Reptiles — a Policy', *British Journal of Herpetology*, 4 (1973), 339-41.

Corbett, K. F., and Tamarind, D. L. 'Conservation of the Sand Lizard, *Lacerta agilis*, by Habitat Management', *British Journal of Herpetology*, 5 (1979), 799-823.

Fitter, R. S. R. *The Ark in Our Midst*. Collins, 1959.

Frazer, D. *Reptiles and Amphibians in Britain*. Collins, 1983.

Frazer, J. F. D. 'The Reptiles and Amphibians of the Channel Islands...', *British Journal of Herpetology*, 1, part 2 (1949), 51-3.

Frazer, J. F. D. 'Introduced Species of Amphibians and Reptiles in Mainland Britain', *British Journal of Herpetology,* 3 (1964), 145-50.

Leighton, G. R. *The Life History of British Lizards*. Morton, 1903.

Lever, C. *The Naturalized Animals of the British Isles*. Hutchinson, 1977.

Prestt, I.; Cooke, A. S.; and Corbett, K. F. 'British Amphibians and Reptiles', pages 229-54 in Systematics Association Special Volume Number 6, *The Changing Flora and Fauna of Britain*. Academic Press, 1974.

Simms, C. *Lives of British Lizards*. Goose and Son, 1970.

Smith, M. A. 'The Wall Lizard in England', *British Journal of Herpetology*, 1 (1951), 99-100.

Smith, M. A. *The British Amphibians and Reptiles*. Collins, fifth edition 1973.

Spellerberg, I. F. 'Britain's Reptile Immigrants', *Country Life*, 20 (1975).

ACKNOWLEDGEMENTS

Illustrations are acknowledged as follows: H. R. Arnold and J. Abblitt (NERC), 4, 8, 15; Eric and David Hosking, 2, 3, 19. All other illustrations are by the author. For various courtesies grateful thanks are also due to I. Davis and M. Preston.